Francis Day

The sacraments

Francis Day

The sacraments

ISBN/EAN: 9783741112287

Manufactured in Europe, USA, Canada, Australia, Japa

Cover: Foto ©Lupo / pixelio.de

Manufactured and distributed by brebook publishing software
(www.brebook.com)

Francis Day

The sacraments

THE SACRAMENTS,

ETC.

THE

SACRAMENTS.

BY THE

REV. MAURICE F. DAY, M.A.,

Incumbent of St. Matthias's Church, Dublin.

DUBLIN:
GEORGE HERBERT, 117, GRAFTON-STREET.
LONDON:
HAMILTON AND CO.; HATCHARD AND CO.

—

1866.

PREFACE.

THESE two Sermons, with the greater portion of the Notes, formed part of a volume of Sermons preached in the ordinary ministry at St. Matthias's Church, and published some time since. I have thought it well to reprint this portion of the volume, and to put it forward in a separate shape, because of the peculiar importance, at the present time, of the subject on which it treats.

Mistaken views, concerning both the Sacraments, have been the source and centre of much unsound teaching within our Church. The view has been put forward concerning Baptism, that all infants who are baptized, without any regard to the sincerity of faith, or earnestness in prayer of those who have presented them—without any respect to the secret will of God, or to any circum-

B

stance whatsoever but the bare fact that they are baptized—are then and there born again of the Holy Ghost.
Views of the Lord's Supper, equally contrary to Scripture and to the teaching of our Reformed Church, have
also been put forward: that there is a peculiar presence
of Christ in the consecrated bread and wine upon the
table; and that these material objects are offered in some
way as a sacrifice to God. On these false views of the
Sacraments I have endeavoured to speak in the Sermons
and still more in the Notes which follow; and I trust,
that enough will be found there, to shew that they are
entirely unwarrantable, and contrary to the teaching both
of the Scriptures and of our Church.

Another view of Baptism, urged very strongly at
present by some who have left the communion of our
Church, is, that we have no right to give baptism to
infants, and that those who have been so baptized ought
to receive baptism again. The minds of some members
of our Church have been disturbed in this way; and it
seems well to restate the grounds on which the Christian
Church, in all ages, has felt warranted in giving baptism,

not only to believers themselves, but to their infant
children. I have referred to this subject in the Sermon,
and stated, very briefly, what I believe to be the
strongest reason of all, why the infant children of Christian parents are entitled to receive baptism.

But it is not merely in reference to these disputed
points, that I feel it important at present to bring forward
the subject of the Sacraments. The danger of such
disputes, of the false views of the Sacraments put forward
by some, and of the denial of infant baptism by others, is
that spiritually-minded Christian people may, in very
weariness, turn away from the matter altogether, and
wish to think and speak but little of the Sacraments. I
believe that such a result would be very unworthy of our
privileges and our position. The abuse of the Sacraments is not to take away their use. They are precious
tokens and means of grace to every true believing soul;
and therefore I have sought in these pages to set forth
their preciousness to those who use them rightly. Each
of the Sacraments may be compared to the ring in mar-
riage. There is no value in that ring itself; it is gene-

rally of the very simplest character. If placed on the
finger of an unmarried woman it would have no meaning
in it; it would only be considered as a very unsuitable
and unseemly ornament. But a wife prizes that ring
above rubies, because it is the pledge and instrument of
a union which only death can sever. And so it is both
with Baptism and the Supper of the Lord. We are not
to look for any mysterious quality in these Sacraments
themselves. Neither are we so grossly to pervert their
use, as to think that the outward sign always conveys, to
every one who receives it, the thing that is signified.
But, while giving no place to any such ideas, one who
believes on the Lord Jesus Christ and loves Him, who
is united to Him by the living work of the Spirit in his
soul, is to look upon the Sacraments as visible pledges
and means of that union—most precious to him as such:
a union which not even death itself can dissolve, but
which shall continue unbroken when time shall be no
more.

BAPTISM.

"And now why tarriest thou? arise and be baptised, and wash away thy sins, calling on the name of the Lord."—Acts, xxii. 16.

THE Christian religion and the Jewish religion are, in many ways, different from one another; but in no way more different than in this—that the Jewish was a most ceremonial religion; the Christian religion has hardly any ceremonies at all, and those which it has, are of the simplest character.

There are two very simple rites appointed as part of the Christian religion—Baptism, and the Lord's Supper. In these, the very commonest things are to be made use of, things which may be easily found in any country, or in any place; water in one of these ordinances, and bread and wine in the other. There is no direction in either case, as to the quantity which is to be made use of, or the posture in which they are to be received; whether the person baptized is to be plunged into water, or the water to be poured upon him; whether the bread and wine in the Lord's Supper is to be received sitting, or standing, or kneeling. These questions, which have been so fiercely disputed among men, are not to be decided by any directions given in Scripture; as if to show us, that it is not the outward act that we are to look to, but the inward and spiritual meaning which belongs to it.

I desire to speak to you, at present, on one of these ordinances, Baptism, and in doing so there are three distinct points, on which I should wish to dwell for a few minutes. First, I would speak of the design and nature of the ordinance in itself, what is its meaning, and for what purpose it was intended. Secondly, I wish to show you that we are warranted in baptizing, not only grown up persons who believe, but also the infant children of Christian parents, before they are capable of believing. And thirdly, I desire to say a few words as to the doctrine of Baptism, set forth in the Articles, and Catechism, and Services of the Church of England. My earnest desire is to consider these things, in a way that may be of practical benefit to us all; that, as we go along, we may see what lessons of instruction, or warning, or encouragement, this subject is fitted to impress upon our hearts.

I. Baptism was appointed by our Lord Jesus Christ, as the means of admitting people, visibly and outwardly, to the company of His disciples. His command concerning it is given at the close of the Gospel of St. Matthew, " Go ye, therefore, and teach all nations, baptizing them in the name of the Father, and of the Son, and of the Holy Ghost." This we find was done by His Apostles, and by all the early preachers of the Gospel whose labours are recorded in the Acts. When the Apostles preached to the multitude on the day of Pentecost (Acts, ii.), and they were converted to the Gospel, they were baptized in that profession. When Philip the Evangelist went down to Samaria (chap. viii.), and preached there, when the people believed they were baptized. When Peter preached to the household of Cornelius (chap. x.), and the Holy Ghost came upon them, they were baptized as disciples of the Lord Jesus. And when Paul and Silas were the means of converting Lydia and the jailer (chap. xvi.) as the first fruits unto God in Philippi, we read concerning each of them, that they were baptized and their households.

But while baptism was thus the means of admitting any persons, visibly, to the company of Christ's disciples; it was also a seal and pledge to those who were truly such, that they were partakers of the blessings of discipleship. It was the sign of admission to the Christian covenant, and so it was a pledge to those who were really admitted to it, that the blessings of the covenant were theirs. Its two great blessings are forgiveness of sins, and a new birth by the power of the Spirit, and all who believe on the Lord Jesus Christ receive those blessings. Baptism is to such, a pledge and assurance that they receive them It is a pledge to all believers, of the forgiveness of their sins. So St. Peter speaks of it (Acts ii. 38), " Repent, and be baptized every one of you in the name of Jesus Christ for the remission of sins." And so it is spoken of likewise in the text, " Arise, and be baptized, and wash away thy sins, calling on the name of the Lord." And it is a pledge to all believers that they are made partakers of a new nature, by the power of the Holy Ghost. So St. Paul seems to speak of it (Rom. vi. 4) when he says, " We are buried with Him by baptism unto death." And again (Coloss. ii. 12), " Buried with Him in baptism, wherein also ye are risen with Him." And our Lord may be considered as referring to baptism as the outward sign and seal of regeneration, in that well-known saying of His (John, iii.), " Except a man be born of water, and of the Spirit, he cannot enter into the kingdom of God."

Baptism is thus, to those who believe on the Lord Jesus, the pledge of their forgiveness, and the outward sign of their being made new creatures by the power of the Holy Ghost. It is not baptism that gives these blessings. We have one undoubted instance in Scripture of a person being saved without being baptized at all—the thief upon the cross. He was, we know, forgiven all his sin. He was likewise born again of the Holy Ghost, and yet he never was baptized. It is not, therefore, baptism that bestows these blessings of salvation upon a person. They are received simply by faith in Jesus Christ; but baptism is the seal and pledge which the Lord Himself has appointed to be given to believers, assuring them of these blessings; and He has appointed it with such authority, that no one is at liberty to neglect it. It is the Lord Himself who says, "He that believeth and is baptized shall be saved." On the other hand, baptism is of no use to unbelievers. It is an empty sign which has no force in it, and which leaves them as dead and destitute of spiritual blessing as they were before.

My brethren, let me say a word upon this head to those, if there are such here present, who are not baptized, and yet are believing on the Lord Jesus as their Saviour. I know that some such have been worshipping with us in times past, and some of them, being convinced of the duty and privilege of baptism, have, I am thankful to say, been baptized in this church; and so it may be that there are some such present here to-day. Now, if you do heartily accept the Lord Jesus Christ to be your Saviour, and if you do believe what the Gospel tells you, that He has reconciled you to God by His blood, then I would say to you in the words of the text, "Why tarriest thou? arise, and be baptized." Why will you not visibly, and openly, in the way which the Lord has appointed, accept that covenant of grace, which with your heart you do inwardly accept? As long as you refuse to be baptized, you refuse to put on the outward mark which the Lord has chosen for His disciples, to distinguish them from others; and you neglect the visible pledge which He has graciously given for the confirming of their faith. ' I cannot imagine how anyone who loves the Saviour, and values His blessed Gospel, can keep back from being baptized in His name.

And to all who believe on the Lord Jesus as their Saviour, and have already been baptized in the profession of that faith, I would say, ever look back upon your baptism, not as a mere ceremony, as some people would treat it, but as a pledge which you have given to the Lord Jesus Christ, and which He has given to you, of the spiritual union which exists, and shall ever hold between your soul and Him. If you were baptized in your infancy, as I suppose most here present were, that does not make any difference. It was the pledge given you beforehand, in the gracious providence of God, that you were one of His elect children; which pledge became effectual, and carried out in your actual experience, when faith was quickened in your soul by the power of the Holy Ghost. Do not be hindered from this view of it, by the thought that many others have been baptized, to whom it is no such pledge of salvation. That is nothing to you. It is a pledge of salvation to believers, and to no others; and the fact of unbelievers being possessed of it, and getting no benefit at all, does not hinder you, as a believer, from getting most precious benefits through its means.

II. This brings us to the second point which I said we would consider—Who are the proper persons to be baptized? Whether we are warranted in baptizing not only grown-up persons who believe, which all are agreed upon, but also the infant children of believers. Now, it is sometimes thought that the question may be settled by asking, Where is the command for baptizing children; or, Where is the plain instance of children, in the New Testament, being baptized? But as to the command, we might well answer, Where is there anything in it, to hinder their being baptized? The Lord's command concerning baptism is that which I have already referred to at the close of St. Matthew's Gospel. He says there, "Go teach [or make disciples of] all nations, baptizing them." There is nothing there to limit the ordinance to those who are grown up; and those who hold to the practice of infant baptism, might argue (as I believe they have), that as " nations " are here spoken of, as being visibly received into the Church; infants, who are a very large part of any nation, must of necessity be received. I would not build anything upon that argument. My own opinion is, that from the command of the Lord, nothing can be argued upon this particular point, either one way or the other. The question,

Where is the command to baptize children, does not settle the point; there is nothing in the command either for or against it.

Again, the question is asked, Where is there any special instance of infants being baptized, in the Acts of the Apostles? That question also leaves the matter as it found it. There are accounts given of baptism in the Acts, which may well be considered as including children. For instance, where it is said (chap. xvi.) that Lydia was baptized, " and her household," and that the jailer was baptized, " he and all his." We cannot prove that children were among them, but neither can it be proved that they were not. But, even if it were clear that all the baptisms mentioned in the Acts, were of grown-up persons who believed, it would not be conclusive; because all agree, that where the Gospel is first preached to any people, it is only grown-up believers that are to be baptized. Until this is first done, there can be no baptizing of children, and even then it is but little mentioned. Read any Report of the Church Missionary Society, and you will find it is the baptisms of grown-up persons that are particularly related in it; those of infants are passed over almost in silence. The question, as to any specific account of the baptism of a child, leaves the matter undecided.

We must, therefore, decide the question upon other grounds; and to my mind, the strong foundation upon which to rest the baptism of infants, is the command given by God Himself, in the Old Testament, concerning that ordinance, which, for the first four hundred years after it was given, seems to have stood in the place of baptism—I mean the rite of circumcision. We all agree that, from the time of Moses down, this was an ordinance of the Jewish law—a badge of obedience to the law; insomuch that the Apostle Paul, in arguing with the Galatians, does not hesitate to say (chap. v. 3), " I testify to every man that is circumcised that he is a debtor to the whole law." But then we are to remember, what our Lord observed to the Jews on one occasion (John, vii. 22), that circumcision, originally, was " not of Moses, but of the fathers." It was given originally to Abraham; and we find the same Apostle Paul bearing witness, that in his case, and, of course, in that of all who lived for four hundred years after, until the time of Moses, it was not an ordinance of the law, but of the Gospel. When it was given to Abraham (Gen. xvii.), God said of it (verse 11), " It shall be a token of the covenant betwixt me and you." Now, what was the covenant which God made with Abraham? We are told (Galatians, iii. 17), " The covenant that was confirmed before of God in Christ." It was the Gospel, the one under which Christians are now living. There is no difference, in that respect, between Abraham and us. It says, in that same chapter (verse 9), " They which be of faith, are blessed with faithful Abraham."

Circumcision, then, as originally given, and as existing afterwards for four hundred years, was the seal, not of the law, but of the Gospel—what baptism is now. And its perfect coincidence with baptism is very strikingly set forth by the same Apostle when speaking of Abraham (Rom. iv. 11), " He received the sign of circumcision, a seal of the righteousness of the faith which he had yet being uncircumcised." That is just what baptism is, to a grown-up person who believes and is baptized, " a seal of the righteousness of faith." And yet we find, while circumcision was thus the seal of the covenant of the Gospel, a pledge of righteousness to the believer, God expressly commanded it to be given to infants ; and so we conclude, by what 1 think is the fairest inference, that it is His will that baptism, which is now what circumcision was then, should also be given to infants. Otherwise, children would be put into an inferior position, in the dealings of God, than ever they were before. When circumcision was the seal of the Gospel covenant, God commanded it to be given to infants. When it became the seal of the legal covenant, He still willed it to be given them. And can we believe that now, when the covenant, which was made with Abraham, has been republished and proclaimed in the Gospel of Christ, the Lord would alter His mode of dealing, and that infants are, for the first time, to be cast out from any visible portion in the covenant.

My brethren, I have dwelt long upon this second point, longer than I intended ; but it is, I believe, a very important subject, and one that I am thus glad to put before you at some length. I wish that you, parents who believe in Christ, should see the warrant which you have for bringing your children, before they know anything, and setting thus the visible seal of the covenant upon them. I look upon those who forbid the baptism of children, as acting very much the same part as the disciples (Mark, x.), when they were sending away the little ones that were brought to the Saviour. They no doubt felt, as these good people do now concerning infant baptism, that it was an unnecessary ceremony, and they rebuked those that brought them. But the Lord did not agree with them in that. He said, Suffer them to come, " and he took them up in His arms, put His hands upon them, and blessed them."

Christian parents, be thankful that the privilege is given you of dedicating your children to the Lord, and of bringing them visibly, as Abraham brought his children, within the bounds of the covenant, and praying that covenant blessings may be given them. But remember, baptism is only the beginning. It is only the seal of all that is to come after. It is not being baptized that will make them safe, but having a living faith in Christ, wrought in their souls by the power of the Holy Ghost. If you bring them to the Lord Jesus in baptism, see that you bring them up for Him in their after life. If you claim this inheritance of spiritual blessing for them at first, let them ever see afterwards, both in what you teach themselves, and in the way in which your own life goes on, that these are the things which you really prize and seek after. It is a blessed thing to baptize the children of believing parents; but it is a profane thing for parents to come professing their own faith, and asking that their children should be baptized into the same, and afterwards to go away and live without Christ themselves, and let their children also grow up without Him. The value of infant baptism is not to be judged from such cases. If you judged any Christian ordinance by the way in which many use it, and by the amount of good which they receive, we might say that everything was profane and useless. We are to judge of them when they are used by Christian people; and so, I say again to Christian parents, thank God for the privilege of being allowed to baptize your little ones, and pray for grace and wisdom to bring them up as those who were baptized.

III. I must say a few words, lastly, as to the doctrine of Baptism, set forth in the formularies of our Church. This is not with the view of showing you what the truth is upon the subject; that can be only known from Scripture, and that I have already endeavoured to set forth ; but, as some have an impression that the Church of England differs from Scripture upon the subject, I would add a few words to remove that impression. When we want to know the doctrine of the Church of England upon any matter, the plain course is to refer to the Articles of Religion. They were drawn up for this very purpose, as the confession of our faith, and of our views upon other important matters. They are plainly fitted for this purpose, in a way that forms of prayer were never fitted or intended. If we wanted to know the religious opinions of a man, we never would think of knowing them by listening to his prayers. We would ask him to state them, in a more direct manner, to ourselves. And so, we are not to gather the doctrines of the Church of England from certain expressions made use of in prayer, when the object in using them may be variously explained; but we are to refer to the Articles of Religion, where those doctrines are clearly and expressly laid down. Now, there is one Article (XXV.) on the Sacraments generally ; and there is another Article (XXVII.) on Baptism in particular. Art. XXV. has this statement generally upon the Sacraments:—" In such only as worthily receive the same, they have a wholesome effect or operation." And Art. XXVII. says in regard to baptism, that it is " a sign of regeneration, whereby they that receive baptism rightly, are grafted into the Church." In both these Articles, it is plainly stated, that baptism is not to be considered as always

c

conveying the blessing along with it, but only when the ordinance is rightly and worthily received. And when we refer to the Catechism of our Church, we have it stated what is the right receiving of baptism:—" Repentance, whereby they forsake sin, and faith, whereby they steadfastly believe the promises of God."

We are to carry these statements with us, in interpreting the language of our baptismal services. Every one allows this to be done in the service for grown-up persons. When the Minister there pronounces the baptized person regenerate, it is, as a matter of course, understood to depend on the sincerity of the profession which has been made; if the repentance and faith which has been professed is actually existing in the person. And so we are to deal with the case of infants also. They are pronounced regenerate; but it is on profession of the repentence and faith, which they are afterwards expected to possess. I do not mean merely on the promise made by sponsors, for that is a human institution; but, as infants are baptized in any communion of Christians, in the hope that they will yet have these things; so it is on the prospect of their having them, that the thanksgiving is offered on their behalf. We may not think it well to have it so expressed. We might think it better to have it so as that no mistake could be made on the matter. But we are not, on that account, to suppose that, in its baptismal service, our Church has departed from what it stated in the Articles; we are to explain the services in conformity with the Articles. And where a person who has been baptized, whether a grown-up person or a child, afterwards shows that he has neither repentance nor faith, we are not to hesitate in saying that he never was regenerated; and I believe, in saying so, we express the true doctrine of the Church of England.

My brethren, I would address you as baptized persons, as almost all here I suppose are such; and I would address you as those who, for the most part at all events, were baptized in your infancy, according to the form of the Church of England. These expectations were acted on concerning you ; these thanksgivings were offered on your behalf. And now, I ask you to consider, on the testimony of your own conscience, whether there has been an actual, substantial carrying out of these things in your own history and experience? Are you really regenerate, by the power of the Holy Ghost? The change is not some obscure and undiscernible thing, so that its effects might wholly disappear, and a person not know whether he was regenerate or not. Our Lord speaks of it as something which is to be known and felt, when he says (John, iii.):—" That which is born of the flesh is flesh, and that which is born of the Spirit is spirit." You are to know whether it has taken place, by those two things which I have just been speaking of—repentance and faith. There is no regeneration, where these are not wrought in the heart by the Holy Ghost. Have you faith in Jesus Christ? Have you received Him as your Saviour? Do you believe in His blood, as having reconciled you to God, and put away your sin? Are you at peace with God now, by resting on the Saviour's righteousness and atonement? And then, have you repentance, whereby sin is forsaken? Has the pardoning mercy of God, which you enjoy in Jesus Christ, led you to hate sin, and to love holiness? Do you count yourself as no longer your own property, but the property of the Lord Jesus Christ; and are you seeking to live for Him, as His servant in the world? My brethren, it is when these things are in us, that we can say we are regenerate. It is when Christ is thus accepted as the Saviour, and when the blessed Spirit stirs us to love Him and to serve Him, that we can say we are made partakers of the blessings of the covenant. The outward seal of baptism has, then, had joined to it the inestimable blessing of spiritual regeneration. But, otherwise, what use is baptism, but the seal of an engagement, which never has been truly entered into; an empty name, which gives no benefit to a person in this life, and which will give him nothing to stand upon, at death or in judgment.

But let me say a word to those who have been baptized, and who fear that their souls have received no blessing, and yet who truly desire to enjoy it. My brethren, take encouragement, from the fact that you were baptized, to come now to God in the name of the Lord Jesus Christ, and to claim for yourself every blessing of the Gospel. Why was it so ordered, in the providence of God, that before you could know anything, the seal of His covenant should thus have been set upon you? What does this say to you, but, Come now and enjoy the blessings of the covenant of grace. Remember that it is a covenant of grace altogether—free and undeserved mercy to sinners, through the redemption that is in Christ Jesus. You are to be justified freely; you are to receive the gift of the Spirit freely; you are daily and yearly, as long as you live, to be receiving fresh renewals of these mercies—free forgiveness of the daily sin that rises up—strength and holiness freely imparted by the blessed Spirit. These are the blessings of the new covenant. Why should any baptized person that really desires them, live one day without their enjoyment? You have less to do, than Saul was told to do in the text. You have been baptized already, and so you do not need to be baptized again. I would, then, just leave out that word, and apply to you the remaining language of the text— " Why tarriest thou? arise, . . and wash away thy sins, calling on the name of the Lord." Look at once at the Lord Jesus, who is the Mediator of the new covenant; and at His blood which speaketh better things than that of Abel. Rest on Him, as having once for all made atonement for your sins, and as being now the Lord your Righteousness. Doubt the Word of God no longer; but on the testimony of that Word, believe that He is at peace with you, when you thus take the Lord Jesus as your Saviour. And it is through this confidence, exercised in the promises of His Word, that the Spirit will work in you all His precious fruits. Love, and joy, and peace, and holy devotedness to the Saviour's service, and a bright hope of seeing Him at His coming—all these will spring from the heartfelt reliance upon God's bare word of promise, and they can spring from nothing else.

THE LORD'S SUPPER.

"And as they were eating, Jesus took bread, and blessed it, and brake it, and gave it to the disciples, and said, Take eat: this is my body. And he took the cup, and gave thanks, and gave it to them saying, Drink ye all of it; for this is my blood of the new testament, which is shed for many for the remission of sins."—St. Matt. xxvi. 26-28.

WE have an account given us here of the first institution of the Lord's Super; and we can see how suitable the occasion was for its institution. The Lord Jesus had met with his disciples, to partake of that great Jewish feast, which was in memory of the wonderful deliverance that God gave His people, when they were coming out of Egypt. The lamb which was on the table, and the unleavened bread beside it, reminded them of that night when the cry was heard throughout the land of Egypt; and when, through the sprinkling of the blood of the lamb, the houses of Israel were preserved from destruction. When the Lord and His disciples were met, in memory of that event, it was a suitable time to appoint another feast, which should come instead of this, as a memorial of a far higher, and more glorious deliverance. It was not a deliverance from temporal death, but a deliverance, for all who should receive it, from the death that is eternal. And as the deliverance which has been wrought, was not only for the Jewish people, but for all the nations of the earth, so this memorial was to be perpetuated among all nations, that all who are made partakers of the blessing, should shew forth, in this way, their gratitude for the blessing which they have received.

There was another reason also, which made this occasion, on which the Lord and His disciples were met, a most suitable time for the appointment of this ordinance. It was the last time that they were to meet after this manner. The Apostle Paul, when speaking of it (1 Cor. xi.), reminds us that it was "the same night in which he was betrayed," that the Lord Jesus instituted this memorial of His death. His enemies had already their plans matured for His end. The chief priests and their officers were looking out. The traitor was about to go forth, to join them at the appointed place. In a few hours, the trial in the High Priest's palace, and the trial, if it might be called such, before the judgment-seat of Pilate, were to be hurried through; the cross was to be set up; and there, on the accursed tree, the adorable Redeemer was to yield up His life as a sacrifice for sin. It was the most suitable time of all, for this memorial of His sacrifice to be appointed.

I. In speaking to you on the subject of the Lord's Supper, I wish, in the first place, to make a few remarks on the language which the Lord here uses in appointing it. He said of the bread which He gave to His disciples, " Take eat, this is my body;" and He said likewise of the cup, " This is my blood of the new testament, which is shed for many for the remission of sins." We, Protestants, are sometimes taunted with not believing the words which our Lord Jesus Christ spoke on this occasion. It is thought by some, that we explain away, or reject these sayings of His which I have just quoted. Now, I say for myself, and I hope every one of us here will be ready to say the same, that on this, as on every other matter, we receive the words of the Lord Jesus in their plain and absolute meaning; and would be sorry, indeed, to set them aside in any way. The Lord said, " This is my body," and " This is my blood:" and I believe that in the fullest and most unqualified manner.

Do you believe then, it might be said, that the bread has been changed into the body of Christ, and that the wine has been changed into His blood? No, I do not; for the Lord never said it. I do not find it written, either in our Bible, or in any version of the Scripture that was ever made, or in the original Greek, that He said, " This is changed into my body," and " This is changed into my blood." If the

Lord did say so, then we would endeavour to believe it; but we may be very thankful that He never said it. What He said was, " This *is* my body." There is no change there. And the meaning of that expression is just what we give to the same word, when He used it at other times. I will refer you to a passage in this same Gospel, where He uses precisely the same expression seven times over, within the space of three verses; and every time that He does so, His meaning is very plain (chap. xiii. 37-39):—" He that soweth the good seed is the Son of man: the field is the world; the good seed are the children of the kingdom; but the tares are the children of the wicked one; the enemy that sowed them is the devil; the harvest is the end of the world; and the reapers are the angels." What is the meaning of the words " is " and " are," in each of the clauses of that passage? Do they mean that the seed sown in the field was changed into living men; and so of the other clauses? We never would think of so extravagant an interpretation. Our Lord meant simply that the one thing represented the other; and that is precisely His meaning in the text. We, Protestants, believe His words most fully, in the sense in which all people understand them in other places, and so in the sense in which they are to be understood here. And it is a way in which we ourselves continually speak. I point to a picture or statue, and say, That *is* the Queen; without ever guarding my words, or supposing it possible that any one can mistake my meaning.

I have said this much, because of the vain attempts which Romanists make, to build a monstrous doctrine on the simple language of the text; and because I know that many here, of all ranks, are likely to come into contact with Roman Catholics. But, there are, sometimes, views and ideas apparently held by members of our own Church, which lean in the same direction, and are destitute of any ground on which to rest. I refer to regarding the bread and wine in the Lord's Supper, as if it had become in some way different from what it was before; or as if there were some presence of the Lord attached to it, after a mysterious manner. Now, there is no presence of the Lord whatever, in that bread and wine, consecrated or unconsecrated. In either case it is just bread and wine, and nothing more. The presence of the Lord is not in that material substance which rests on the table, which the officiating minister gives to the worshipper, and which he eats and drinks. It is in the soul of the believer that He is present. It is the manifestation of Christ to the soul, by the Spirit, and through the exercise of faith, that is His presence. We know of no other way in which the Lord is present, but that way. It is the same kind of presence that is always in the soul of a believer; but we may look for a special and increased enjoyment of it, when we are keeping rightly, and humbly, and believingly, this ordinance which the Lord has appointed us to keep. I believe it is very important for us, to have clear ideas upon this point. The want of them has led to ways of speaking and acting, very inconsistent with the principles of our Reformed Church. It is a wrong direction entirely for our minds to be turned in; it is not thus that we shall receive any spiritual edification. It will draw us away from seeking that presence of Christ in our souls, which alone can give blessing; and it will send us to look for something, which has no existence except in our own imagination.

II. When we look upon the bread and wine, which the Lord commanded to be received, simply as representations and symbols of His blessed body and blood, then we can understand and enter into the meaning of the ordinance ; and those who believe on the Lord Jesus Christ as their Saviour, can draw near and partake of it with comfort. We are first to consider, what it is that believers do, in coming to the table. Our Lord's own words, as given in the Gospel of St. Luke, tell us what they are to do. His command was, " Do this in remembrance of me." And the well-known passage (1 Cor. xi.) sets forth, fully, the spirit in which this memorial is to be kept—" As often as ye eat this bread, and drink this cup, ye do shew the Lord's death till he come." When we come to this ordinance, we proclaim the death of the Lord Jesus Christ. We tell it abroad publicly, and on every side, as the great event in which our salvation is concerned, and as the great object upon which our faith is set.

When we come to the Lord's Supper, we show forth or proclaim the death of the Lord Jesus Christ, as a great event which once took place, of immense and infinite importance to the world. The bread and wine are placed upon the table, in token of His body and blood, separate from one another, and so betokening His death. Moreover, the bread is broken, and the wine poured into the cup, in remembrance of His death brought about by violence. " This is my blood which is shed," is the Lord's saying in the text; and "this is my body which is broken for you," are part of His words as given by the Apostle Paul.

But it is not the Lord's death merely as a martyr, or witness to the truth, that is here to be remembered. He tells us Himself in the text in what light we are to regard the shedding of His blood—" This is my blood of the new testament, which is shed for many for the remission of sins." It is in this way that His death is to be regarded, at all times, as of such importance. By His death, the blessings of the new covenant have been obtained. It is thus expressed (Heb. ix. 15), " For this cause he is the mediator of the new testament, that by means of death, for the redemption of the transgressions that

were under the first testament, they which are called
might receive the promise of eternal inheritance." This
is the light in which the death of the Lord Jesus Christ
is continually presented to us in Scripture; and it is in
this character that we proclaim His death, when we
come to this feast that He has appointed. We tell in
the face of the world, by means of this solemn memorial, the stupendous sacrifice which God has provided
for the taking away of sin. It is true that this memorial is kept up, by those who deny the atoning sacrifice
of the Son of God. It is hard to think for what purpose they can keep it. If the death of the Lord was not
an atoning sacrifice for sin, why should it be so specially
remembered? In such a case, His life as a teacher and
example, is far more worthy of remembrance than His
death. It was of far greater importance to the world.
But the Lord's own words in the institution of this
ordinance, carry with them the condemnation of all
such views. He said, " This is my blood, which is
shed *for the remission of sins*." That is the true way in
which His death is to be regarded.

But, in showing forth the Lord's death, in this ordinance, we not only declare it to be the great atonement
which God has provided for sin; we make, as regards
ourselves personally, a profession of our faith in that
atonement. The bread and wine are not only placed
upon the table, but each individual comes forward and

partakes of these things as they are given him. This is a confession made by the person himself, before his fellow-Christians, that he has trusted in the death of the Lord Jesus Christ for his salvation, and taken Him to be his Saviour and Redeemer. This is the confession which is made by those who come to the table of the Lord. And how joyful is that confession! There is no rejoicing in ourselves; we come humbled in the very dust as sinners. The declaration which we make as regards our own goodness is this: " We are not worthy, so much as to gather up the crumbs under thy table." But, while we are humbled as regards ourselves, all who come declare in doing so, that they have trusted in the Lord Jesus Christ for salvation, and that in Him they have found forgiveness. This is a happy acknowledgment to make, and it is one which the Lord Jesus calls upon all to make, who have found deliverance and blessing at His hands. This is one of the ways in which you are to glorify the name of the Lord Jesus Christ. It is a confession which He looks for from you; and, as I have said already, think of what a privilege it is! How happy that believers on the Lord Jesus should thus meet together, and confess to one another, in this ordinance, the blessings of which their Lord has made them to be partakers!

There is one other way, in which we show forth the Lord's death in this ordinance. We proclaim here, in

the sight of all men, that we are the followers of a cruci-
fied Redeemer. We are told (Gal. i.) that when the
Lord Jesus Christ " gave himself for our sins," He did
so in order " that he might deliver us from the present
evil world;" and (Titus, ii.) that He " gave himself for
us, that he might redeem us from all iniquity, and purify
unto himself a peculiar people, zealous of good works."
Therefore, when we proclaim the Lord's death as our
confidence, and the cause of our salvation, we declare
our desire, also, that this object of His death should be
carried out in us; that we should be delivered from this
evil world, purified from all sin, and zealous in good
works. My brethren, this is a profession which all
undoubtedly make who come to the table of the Lord;
a profession not merely of morality, and attention to the
outward forms of religion; but the heartfelt, earnest
purpose to be the property of Christ altogether, to live as
His servants, to love Him, and to glorify His name.
These are the words which we all use, when kneeling
together after having partaken of the ordinance—" Here
we offer and present unto thee ourselves, our souls, and
bodies, to be a reasonable, holy, and lively sacrifice
unto thee." Let no one think lightly of this, because he
sees others going through it who appear to think little of
the matter. What others may do, is not the standard
for you to take. You declare in coming here, that you
desire to follow the Lord Jesus Christ altogether, and

let there be meaning in what you say. And then, if this
is indeed your desire and choice; if you can appeal to
the Searcher of hearts and say, " Lord, thou knowest all
things, thou knowest that I love thee;" and if your
choice is only to consult His will, and to please Him
and not man, then, do not let the feeling of your own
weakness keep you away. The Lord will give you
strength. If He has given you forgiveness of sin
through His blood, He will also carry on the work of
His Spirit in your heart.

III. Having thus seen what it is that believers on the
Lord Jesus Christ do, in coming to the Lord's Supper;
we are to consider, on the other hand, what it is that the
Lord imparts to them, when they come there. We are
told this in the words of Scripture (1 Cor. x. 16), " The
cup of blessing which we bless, is it not the communion
of the blood of Christ? The bread which we break, is
it not the communion of the body of Christ?" The
Lord's Supper is there said to be the communion, or
partaking, of the body and blood of the Lord. This does
not mean any partaking of those things in themselves,
or in their substance. I have shown you already, in
speaking on the words of institution, how there is no
room for supposing such a thing as that; and if we could,
by any extraordinary transmutation, partake bodily of
those things in themselves, how could the soul be bene-
fitted by doing so? What believers do partake of, in the

D

Lord's Supper, are the benefits purchased by the Lord's body and blood, offered for them upon the cross. The benefits and blessings flowing from the sacrifice of Christ, are what is meant by the partaking of His body, and the partaking of His blood. You may consider the language to be peculiar, but I think you will see one occasion at least, in which we are accustomed to use language in the same way. We know that the sun is set high in the heavens, millions of miles distant from this world; yet we continually speak of letting the sun into a room, or shutting the sun out of it, meaning thereby the rays of light and heat proceeding from the sun. It is the same kind of expression that is used, when we are said to partake of the body and blood of the Lord. We partake of them, in the only way in which it is possible, or of any use for us to do so, when we partake of the benefits purchased by His blessed body and blood, offered for us as a sacrifice for sin. Every benefit which comes from that sacrifice, comes down upon the souls of believers in Him, as the rays of the noonday sun come down upon him who is standing underneath them. This is the way in which we are said to partake of the Lord's body and blood, in that passage which I quoted from 1 Cor. x.; and this is what is meant in the saying of our Catechism, which is copied from that passage, " The body and blood of Christ, which are verily and indeed taken and received by the faithful in the Lord's Supper." The precious benefits of His death, are the things of which the faithful, or believers, are actually made to be partakers.

But in what way is it that the Lord's Supper imparts these benefits to the soul of the believer? It is as a seal and pledge of the promises of God made to him in the Gospel. It is when the promises of God in Jesus Christ are first received into the heart, and laid hold upon by faith, that this ordinance which the Lord has appointed, comes as a further assurance to the believer, of the blessings which the promises convey. Such a one coming to the table of the Lord, has a right thus to think within himself. My Lord died for me upon the cross. He there gave Himself a ransom for my soul. He shed His blood for the remission of my sins. He sent to me His word of promise, telling me that, believing on Him, I should receive that forgiveness. I believe His Word. I have trusted in Him as my Saviour and Redeemer. I believe that He has put away my sins, and that they shall never be brought up in judgment against me. And now He has, in His adorable condescension, left me this visible pledge, to be a strengthening of my faith, and a further assurance of His love. My brethren, if we can come to the table of the Lord in this spirit, and with this living, personal faith in Him as our Saviour, we shall surely carry a blessing away. There is no undue exalting of the sacrament in this. There is no expecting it to work of itself, after some mysterious manner, we cannot tell how. It is a simple, intelligible matter. We can see how our faith can be strengthened, and our love increased, and so every spiritual principle stirred within us, by means of this ordinance which the Lord has left. And I believe that it is, when used in this simple, intelligible way, that it is really profitable to the soul. May God enable us always thus to use it, and make it a rich channel of spiritual blessing to every believing soul amongst us.

This is the twofold view, which it is important for us to take, of the Sacrament of the Lord's Supper. It is, on our part, a thankful memorial of the death of Christ. We shew forth His death, as the one atonement for sin. We declare that we ourselves have trusted in it for our salvation; and we profess our solemn purpose henceforth to live wholly unto the Lord. And then it is, on the other hand, given from the Lord to us, as a sure and effectual pledge, that, as believers in Him, we are partakers of all the benefits which His death has purchased.

My brethren, every time that the Lord's Supper is ministered amongst us, it comes as a test to each, calling on us to declare whether or not we are partakers of these things. If we come to the table of the Lord, we declare that we are partakers of them; that the Lord Jesus Christ is ours, and that we are His. That is a happy confession to make, if our conscience bears us witness that it is true. We, ministers of religion, are not the judges; it is well that we are not. We say to every one in the language of Scripture, "Let a man examine himself, and so let him eat of that bread and drink of that cup." But if people are afraid of this self-examination, and go away from the table of the Lord, what do they declare? We have no part in Christ; we have not been reconciled to God by Him; we are not saved through His redemption, and we do not intend to be His servants.

This ordinance shuts us up to decide, concerning our state one way or the other—I mean as far as the profession is concerned; and so it reminds us of this great fact, that we must, in reality, be either one thing or the other. It is a great and solemn truth to think of, that we all are either saved in Christ, and heirs of eternal life in Him; or we are in our lost condition out of Christ, and continuing so, are journeying on to an eternity without hope. This we must all allow, undoubtedly, to be the case. There is no state between the two. True Christians, or mere professors of Christianity; born of the Spirit, or still dead in trespasses and sins; accepted in Christ, or still under God's sentence of condemnation; we must all be in either the one or the other of these states. My brethren, what is any question which concerns us, compared with the infinite consequences which follow upon which of these two conditions we belong to? In a few years it will be of little consequence to you and me, whether we were rich or poor, learned or unlearned; whether our lot in life was prosperous or the contrary; in what region of the world our life was spent, or whether that life itself was of long or short duration? But this will be of infinite and over-powering consequence to us throughout eternity — whether we belonged truly to the Lord Jesus Christ, and were made partakers of the salvation which He has purchased. Let us, then, decide this question without delay. If we are truly some of the Lord's people, then it is for our own happiness, and for the honour of His name, that we be sure upon the matter; and if we are not His, if we have been deceiving ourselves with a name and nothing more, then it is well to know it, and to look at the solemn truth, because the door of entrance into God's favour is still open. The Lord Jesus Christ is that door. There is mercy, and blessing, and pardon, and holiness, for every sinner who will come to God through Him.

NOTES.

Baptism.

"BAPTISMAL Regeneration" seems a phrase very ill-adapted to express the doctrines commonly intended to be conveyed by it. Sometimes it is explained as meaning only that all baptized persons are admitted, in virtue of their baptism, to a certain standing and consequent responsibility. If this be the meaning, I suppose there are few ministers or members of our Church, or perhaps of any Christian communion, who would care to deny the fact; but most of them would question whether it is a right use of language to apply the term in this way. "Regeneration" means a being born again; and our Church marks out very distinctly what is meant, by calling it in one of the Collects of the Baptismal Service, "spiritual regeneration." Moreover, we pray in another part of the Service, "Give thy Holy Spirit to this infant, that he may be born again." And, in the Service for grown-up persons, the portion of Scripture which is read is from the Lord's discourse with Nicodemus (John, iii.), plainly identifying the regeneration which is looked for in baptism, with the great change which the Lord there says must take place in every human being, or "he cannot enter into the kingdom of

God." The admission of all baptized persons, whether in infancy or of full age, to certain privileges and responsibilities in virtue of their baptism, has been called, in technical language, the baptismal *character ;* but to apply the term " regeneration " to it, as that word is used in the Baptismal Services of our Church, seems altogether unwarrantable.

Again : the word regeneration is used by others in its true meaning—as a new birth, or an implanting of a new spiritual life in the soul ; but there are few, if any, of those who profess to hold the doctrine of Baptismal Regeneration, who would assert, that all persons who are baptized, are in this meaning of the word regenerate. They would not affirm that an infidel, coming for some worldly object, and professing his faith in Christ, is spiritually regenerated because he is baptized. I suppose there are few ministers or members of our Church who would affirm this to be the case. Therefore they do not hold that all baptized persons have been necessarily regenerated. " Baptismal regeneration " is thus too large an expression for them to use : what they really mean, and the point of doctrine which they maintain is, that all *infants* are spiritually regenerated in baptism.

Now, the grand objection which occurs, *prima facie,* to such an assertion is, that it makes baptism in the case of infants a different thing from what it is to those who are grown up. With grown-up persons, it is a means and pledge of blessing to all who repent and believe the Gospel : with infants, it is by this doctrine made an invariable means and pledge of blessing to all who are baptized, without any condition or qualification at all. This is a very serious alteration ; and the question naturally arises,

On what authority does it rest? Certainly not on Scripture. The strong expressions (and they are very strong) which are used in the New Testament concerning baptism, refer directly to the baptism of grown-up persons believing in the Saviour. If these expressions, so employed, do not compel us to believe that all grown-up persons are regenerated in baptism, why should they make us assert that all infants are so regenerated? Where in Scripture is this superiority given to infant baptism above that of adults? And if it is not given in Scripture, neither is it in the teaching of our Church. The Article on baptism (XXVII.) is drawn up chiefly with regard to the case of grown-up persons. This is plain from the expression, " Faith is confirmed, and grace is increased." The baptism of infants is brought in at the end of the Article in a very moderate way. " The baptism of young children is in anywise to be retained in the Church as most agreeable with the institution of Christ." Here would be the place to introduce the assertion, that " All infants are regenerate in baptism ;" but no such assertion is made upon the subject. There is no laying down any doctrine of infant baptism as distinct from the doctrine concerning adults. And as regards the Services of the Church, the same thing is to be said. If it is declared of an infant after its baptism, " Seeing now, dearly beloved brethren, that this child is regenerate," it is declared equally of grown-up persons, " Seeing now, dearly beloved brethren, that these persons are regenerate." And if these expressions, being used in the latter case, do not compel us to believe the universal regeneration of baptized adults, neither does their use in the former case imply our belief in the regeneration of all infants who are baptized.

A dictum has, indeed, been gravely uttered by some divines of our Church, that because infants *place no obstacle* to the grace of baptism, therefore they must all of necessity be regenerated. This is a very amiable belief; but the plain question arises, Where is the ground for such a belief in either the Scriptures, or the documents of the Church of England? On the contrary, it seems directly set aside by one part of the teaching of our Church. After stating in the Catechism that the things which are required in persons to be baptized are " Repentance, whereby they forsake sin, and faith, whereby they steadfastly believe the promises of God," the question is put, " Why, then, are infants baptized, when by reason of their tender age they cannot perform them?" Here would be the place to declare, "Infants receive the blessing, because they place no obstacle in the way." But such is not the answer. Our Church does not draw any such distinction between infants and those who are grown up; it puts them just on the same footing, and meets this difficulty which is suggested, by the answer, "Because they promise them both [repentance and faith] by their sureties, which promise, when they come to age, themselves are bound to perform." This places our Catechism in harmony with the Article and the Services, making no difference between the case of infants and those who are grown up.

Reference is sometimes made to the answer at the opening of the Catechism—" Baptism, wherein I was made a member of Christ, the child of God, and an inheritor of the kingdom of heaven." But the question is to be asked, By whom is this answer supposed to be made? By a young person preparing for confirmation—see the title of the Catechism—a young person who, when asked just after, does he consider himself bound to follow what his sponsors had promised, answers, " Yes, verily, and by God's help, so I will," and who, at the end of the Creed, declares that he is one of " the elect people of God," sanctified by the Holy Ghost. Now, undoubtedly, such a one may well say, that in baptism he was made a member of Christ, a child of God, and an inheritor of the kingdom of heaven, because, whether spiritual life was given then, or it may not be until years after, baptism was the visible act by which these blessings were handed over to all God's " elect people." Election, in our Church's teaching, does not mean election to mere external privileges, but it means election to everlasting life, carried out effectually by the power and love of God. See Article XVII.—" They which be endued with so excellent a benefit of God, be called according to God's purpose, by His Spirit working in due season ;" and so it traces on their course, until " at length, by God's mercy, they attain to everlasting felicity." Those who can claim to be " the elect people of God " after this fashion— and it is such that are supposed to answer the questions of the Catechism—may well repeat, concerning their baptism, the language that is used at the beginning.

When this opinion, that all infants who are baptized have been spiritually regenerated, is attempted to be forced upon us as the doctrine of our Church, it is well, in addition to what has been said, to remember that a formal decision has been taken upon the subject. In the celebrated Gorham case, it was settled by the highest authority, that such an opinion is not required to be held by a clergyman of the Church of England. The legal decision did not go beyond that ; but, the investigation of the subject, and some valuable works which appeared at the time in connection with the controversy, shew that such an opinion is not only not required by our Church, but is contrary to the views of those who drew up her Articles and Services. It is rather hard, after all this, that many should still quietly assume that this opinion is our Church's doctrine, and that those who do not hold it are unfaithful to her teaching.

This doctrine of the regeneration of all infants who are baptized, is supposed, by some, to give honour to the ordinance. So far from doing so, it greatly lowers our idea of its blessings. It teaches us to expect much less in baptism than the Scripture warrants us to expect. It supposes a kind of life to be given to baptized infants, which in most cases fades away, and is never visible at all. If we look on baptism as the seal of the New Covenant, we are to expect something very different from that. We are to look that the person baptized, whether in infancy or riper years, should be made an heir of blessings never to be revoked ; the forgiveness of sin ; the indwelling of the Spirit ; a union with Christ which neither life nor death shall sever. We pray for this, we expect this. If it does not appear, we hope that it may yet be manifested ; but we will not lower the privilege of baptism and of the Gospel, by asserting that some kind of blessing was given which no one ever saw, and which produces no one practical result.

This subject might be pursued to a far greater length. To those who desire to see it considered in a complete and masterly manner, there are two works on the subject which I venture strongly to recommend. One published some years ago, " The Doctrine of the Church of England as to the effects of Baptism in the case of Infants," by W. Goode, D.D., Dean of Ripon. The other, of recent date, which discusses the whole subject of baptism, with the fruits of very extensive reading on the subject, and with a singular amount of calmness and impartiality, "A Review of the Baptismal Controversy," by J. B. Mozley, B.D., Vicar of Old Shoreham, late Fellow of Magdalen College, Oxford.

The Lord's Supper.

It has been declared by some, with apparent humility and reverence, that they would not venture to say what there is in the sacrament; that is, in the bread and wine after it is consecrated. Now if this be humility, it is "a voluntary humility," and if it is reverence, it is reverence that is ill-directed. Our Church ventures to say very plainly what is there: "these thy creatures of bread and wine." And although it might be objected that these expressions are used before the consecration takes place, yet it says that this is what they are when we are "receiving" them, and they are called by that name to the very end of the Service. When the direction is given at the end, that the consecrated bread and wine shall not be carried out of the church, it is in order to prevent a superstitious use of it. This appears from the declaration of Article XXVIII., "The sacrament of the Lord's Supper was not by Christ's ordinance *reserved*, carried about, lifted up or worshipped."

The body and blood of the Lord, which believers partake of in the Lord's Supper, are the same benefits of the death of Christ, of which at other times they are made to be partakers. The Lord's Supper is a means of their partaking of these; not

by any mysterious power contained in it, but because, as a pledge
of the Lord's love, and a seal of His covenant, it stirs up faith
in the soul, and brings it into lively exercise.   This is implied
by our Church in the words made use of, when the bread is delivered into the hand of the communicant.   There are two distinct sentences then repeated; composed at different times, though
afterwards joined together.   The first is a prayer, "The body
of our Lord Jesus Christ which was given for thee, preserve thy
body and soul unto everlasting life."   This is a prayer for the
benefits of the death of Christ to be communicated to the soul.
The second part is an exhortation, "Take and eat this, in remembrance that Christ died for thee, and feed on Him in thine
heart by faith with thanksgiving."   While the bread given by
the minister is to be eaten in remembrance of the Lord's atoning
death, the believer, who receives it, is to feed upon Christ Himself, in his heart by faith.   How is he to do this?   In the same
way in which he always does it.   By looking to what the Lord
did and suffered for him; by resting on the promises of His
Word, assuring himself of their performance.   But it may be
said, Are we not to feed on Him at that very moment when we
are partaking of the bread?   Certainly, and the partaking of
that bread in His name is a great help to our doing so, seeing
that it is the visible token of His covenant which the Lord
Himself has appointed.   But our partaking of Christ then, is in
the same mode and by the same kind of faith, that we partake
of Him at other times.   That this is the doctrine of our Church,
is, I think, very plainly shown by a Rubric in the Service for
the Communion of the Sick.   It says there, that if a man is
prevented by any sufficient cause from receiving the communion,
" the curate shall instruct him, that if he do truly repent him of

his sins, and steadfastly believe that Jesus Christ hath suffered death upon the cross for him, and shed His blood for his redemption, earnestly remembering the benefits he hath thereby, and giving Him hearty thanks therefor, *he doth eat and drink the body and blood of our Saviour Christ profitably to His soul's health, although he do not receive the sacrament with his mouth.*"

Another false view concerning the Lord's Supper, which is now put forward in our Church is, that the bread and wine which are made use of are offered, in some way, as a sacrifice to God. In harmony with this, the communion-table is called an altar, and the ministers of our Church are spoken of as sacrificing priests. Of all this there is not a trace to be found either in our Articles or Services. Anything which seemed like a sacrifice in the Lord's Supper, has been carefully erased from the Prayerbook as we now possess it. The word "altar" has been wholly expunged, and is nowhere to be found within the book. Moreover, it has been decided by legal authority in more than one case brought to trial, that an altar is not allowed in any place of worship belonging to the Church of England. And, to shew how totally different is the character of our priests from the sacrificing priesthood of Rome, it is enough to refer to the language of the Ordination Service. In the Romish Church the sacramental vessels are put into the hands of the person just ordained, with the awful words, "Take thou authority to offer sacrifice to God, and to celebrate masses for the living and the dead." In the Ordination Service of the Church of England there is no mention of a sacrifice at all. Nothing of the kind is referred to. But THE BIBLE is put into the hands of the person who has been ordained a priest, saying, "Take thou authority to preach the Word of God, and to minister the holy Sacraments." If anything of a sacrificing character were assumed as belonging to the presbyters of our Church, this would be the place in which it should be mentioned.

I believe that it is not lowering in any way this blessed ordinance of the Lord's Supper, but raising it to its true character, when we put aside the mysterious ideas in which men have wrapped it up; and when we take it, as set forth in Scripture, and as our Reformed Church has received it, as *a thankful memorial* of the Lord's death; as *a seal and pledge* to each believer, of the blessings which the Gospel has already conveyed to his soul; and as *a means* of conveying those blessings more fully, by stirring up his faith into lively exercise upon the redeeming work of Christ, and upon the gracious promises of God in Him.

I have mentioned two books as worthy of being studied in connection with a single view of the Baptismal subject. I feel it necessary to commend only one book on the subject of the Lord's Supper, because it is so comprehensive in its character as to include all points of view, in which this Sacrament needs to be considered—I mean the great work of Archbishop Cranmer on the Lord's Supper, now so easy of access among the valuable publications of the Parker Society. When we read this book, written by the leader of the English Reformation, plain in language and perfectly intelligible in its views, there can be no doubt left in our minds as to what is the doctrine of the Lord's Supper, as it is held and taught by the Reformed Church of England.

www.ingramcontent.com/pod-product-compliance
Lightning Source LLC
Chambersburg PA
CBHW022042080426

42733CB00007B/939